01/18   lexile 540

FOLLOW THAT BOTTLE!
A PLASTIC RECYCLING JOURNEY

BY BRIDGET HEOS · ILLUSTRATED BY ALEX WESTGATE

AMICUS ILLUSTRATED
is published by Amicus
P.O. Box 1329, Mankato, MN 56002
www.amicuspublishing.us

Paperback edition printed by RiverStream Publishing in arrangement with Amicus.
ISBN 978-1-62243-356-8 (paperback)

LIBRARY OF CONGRESS CATALOGING-IN-PUBLICATION DATA
Names: Heos, Bridget, author. | Westgate, Alex, illustrator.
Title: Follow that bottle! : a plastic recycling journey / by Bridget Heos ; illustrated by Alex Westgate.
Description: Mankato, MN : Amicus, [2017] | Series: Keeping cities clean | Series: Amicus
illustrated | Audience: K to grade 3. | Includes bibliographical references and index.
Identifiers: LCCN 2015047977 (print) | LCCN 2015048854 (ebook) |
ISBN 9781607539643 (library binding) | ISBN 9781681510828 (eBook)
Subjects: LCSH: Plastic scrap—Recycling—Juvenile literature. | Plastics industry and trade—Recycling—Juvenile
literature. | Refuse and refuse disposal—Juvenile literature. | Recycling (Waste, etc.)—Juvenile literature.
Classification: LCC TD798 .H47 2017 (print) | LCC TD798 (ebook) | DDC 363.72/88—dc23
LC record available at http://lccn.loc.gov/2015047977

EDITOR: Rebecca Glaser
DESIGNER: Kathleen Petelinsek

PRINTED in the United States of America at
Corporate Graphics in North Mankato, Minnesota.

HC 10 9 8 7 6 5 4 3 2
PB 10 9 8 7 6 5 4 3 2 1

ABOUT THE AUTHOR
Bridget Heos lives in Kansas City with her husband and four children. She has written more than 80 books for children, including several about the Earth and the environment. Find out more about her at www.authorbridgetheos.com.

ABOUT THE ILLUSTRATOR
Alex Westgate is an illustrator, designer, and artist from Toronto, Ontario, Canada. He has worked for *The Washington Post*, BBC, *Reader's Digest*, and more. He drinks tap water, recycles, and throws things in the garbage every day.

Ah! That water was refreshing! Toss your bottle into the recycling bin—not the trash. Have you ever wondered what happens to the bottle? Let's follow it and find out!

Here comes the truck! This one uses a mechanical arm to pick up the bin. Into the hopper the water bottle goes! Inside, it gets jumbled up with other recyclable items. Then they are smashed to make more room.

All full! Time to visit the recycling facility. First stop: the tipping floor.

Here, the water bottle is pushed onto a conveyor belt. Bottles ride along with paper, cardboard, aluminum, and glass. Workers and machines sort the items.

First, workers set aside big plastic things, like toys, buckets, and laundry baskets.

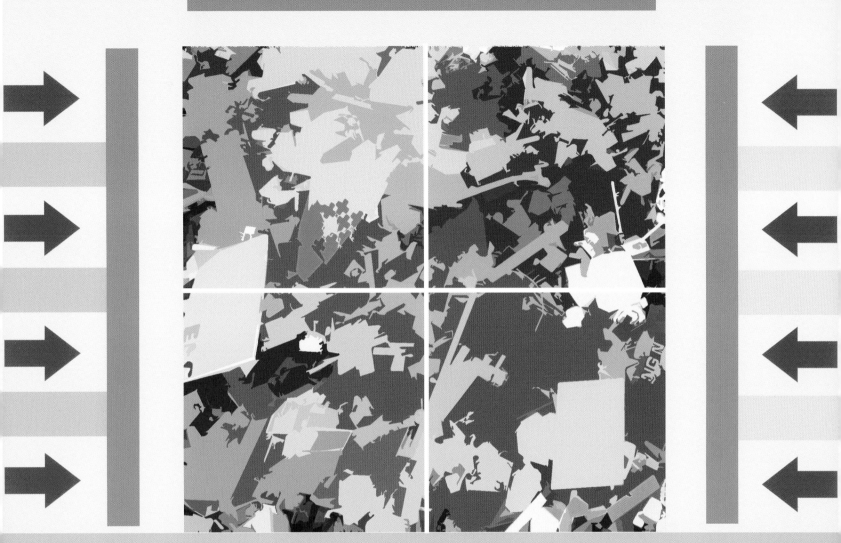

The large items are pressed into a big cube and tied with rope. This is called a bale. Bales will be made from each type of recyclable.

Plastic recyclables are separated by number. Plastic bottles are number I plastic. Yes, that does mean the best! That's because plastic bottles can easily be made into other things.

WE'RE NUMBER ONE!

The water bottle is dumped into a bin with the other plastic bottles.
They go into a compactor and are smashed together into a bale.

Each water bottle is light, but the bale is heavy. It weighs more than 1,300 pounds (590 kg)! The plastic bales are now shipped to different places.

Some bottles are shipped to China. They are melted down and turned into polyester. This fiber becomes carpets, T-shirts, teddy bear stuffing, and more.

WELCOME TO
PLASTIC
WORLD

Other bottles stay in North America. That means less energy is used for shipping. The water bottle goes to a plastic bottle plant, where hundreds of thousands of bottles arrive every day!

I USED TO BE CLEAN. NOW I'M REALLY CLEAN!

First, the bottles get washed. Some bottles held pop or juice, so they're pretty sticky. Machines remove labels and caps. As the bottles are cleaned, they lose 30 percent of their weight.

Now the bottles are shredded into small flakes. They are melted down and then chopped into tiny pellets. Like grain, the pellets are stored in silos.

19

Next, the pellets are shipped to bottle makers.

The pellets are made into new bottles.

Wow, the water bottle is a water bottle again!

It can be recycled over and over!

RECYCLE IT YOURSELF
PLASTIC BOTTLE BIRD FEEDER

Even if you don't have recycling facilities where you live, you can use plastic bottles to make other things. With an adult's help, you can make a bird feeder from 100 percent reused materials.

What You Need:

- Used water bottle
- Used wooden chopstick
- Used piece of paper
- Scissors or knife (to be used by an adult)
- Recycled string or ribbon
- Birdseed

What You Do:

1. Near the bottom of the bottle, cut two small holes on opposite sides of the bottle. They should be just big enough for the chopstick.
2. Insert the chopstick so it sticks out on both sides of the bottle. The stick is the birds' perch.
3. Two inches (5 cm) above the perch, cut two ½-inch (1.25 cm) diameter holes. This is where the birds will get the seed.
4. Make a funnel with the paper, and put it over the bottle opening.
5. Pour in the birdseed. (This should be done outside, as a little will spill out of the food holes.)
6. Put the cap on the bottle to keep out the rain.
7. Tie the string around the top of the bottle and hang up your bird feeder!

GLOSSARY

bale A bundle of material pressed and tied together.

compactor A machine that smashes recyclables so they take up less space.

fiber A thin strand of material used to make other items.

mechanical arm A metal claw that lifts up a bin so that it can be emptied into the truck.

pellet A small, rounded unit of a material.

polyester A manufactured fiber used to make clothing and other things.

recyclable An item that can be remade into new things.

silo A tower used for storage.

READ MORE

Bullard, Lisa. **Choose to Reuse**. Minneapolis: Millbrook Press, 2012.

Ditchfield, Christin. **The Story Behind Plastic**. Chicago: Heinemann Library, 2012.

LePetit, Angie. **Trash Magic: A Book About Recycling a Plastic Bottle**. North Mankato, Minn.: Capstone Press, 2013.

Spilsbury, Louise. **Recycling & Reusing**. New York: PowerKids Press, 2015.

WEBSITES

EPA: Recycle City
http://www3.epa.gov/recyclecity/mainmap.htm
Learn about recycling by exploring this cyber city.

Kids Be Green
http://www.kidsbegreen.org/
Find out how to reuse items around the house and play recycling games.

NASA Climate Kids: Recycle This!
http://climatekids.nasa.gov/recycle-this/
Test your knowledge with this recycling game.

PBS Kids: Eeko World
http://pbskids.org/eekoworld/
Follow along with Cheeko and other characters to learn about the recycling process, the environment, and how to take care of the Earth.

Every effort has been made to ensure that these websites are appropriate for children. However, because of the nature of the Internet, it is impossible to guarantee that these sites will remain active indefinitely or that their contents will not be altered.